SCATTERED WITH GRACE

Other Books by Richard Lister

Poetry

Edge & Cusp - Coverstory books, 2022

Non-Fiction

Flourish: Fuller life for all through Church and Community Transformation - Regnum Books, 2023

RICHARD LISTER

SCATTERED WITH GRACE

First published in paperback format by Coverstory books, 2024

ISBN 978-1-0686701-7-6

Copyright © Richard Lister 2024

The right of Richard Lister to be identified as the author of this work has been asserted by him in accordance with the Copyright, Designs and Patents Act 1988.

The cover image is a photograph taken by Richard Lister © 2024

All rights reserved.

No part of this publication may be reproduced, circulated, stored in a system from which it can be retrieved, or transmitted in any form without the prior permission of the publisher in writing.

www.coverstorybooks.com

With grateful thanks to my fellow Mole Valley Poets for your insights and encouragement over the years.

Contents

Simple, calloused feet

Daughter, wandering..5
Turner's flight 6
The sound of hot sap 7
Bulgari's hands 9
A month's kisses...10
Your calloused feet 11
So much depends...12
Hour upon the stage..14

Strange fish

Stamp collectors are a strange 17
There's no smoke for the fool..19
Neptune's Horses 21
A dragon loves 22
Not what they seem...23
Love, hate, punctuate 24
Perukes and periwigs 25
Do we fight 26

Breeze blocks for a heart

Vanishing Point 29
Apart 30
Translating into Russian...32
Give me a child 33
Instinct 34
Wrapped 35
Checkpoint..37
This teetering moment..38

Tantalising flame

In their wake 41
On the cusp..42
What lies ahead..43
Still point..44
Still life?..45
Lasting Difference..46
Can we not pray 47
Let there be lights..48

Beauty for ashes

Intertwined 51
Helix and the Quirk 52
Seen 53
Through silence 54
Girl in a headscarf 55
After your wheelchair 56
What caught me out 57
Cracked 58

❂

Acknowledgements 61

Simple, calloused feet

Daughter, wandering

You are a coracle in the sea:
framework of split and interwoven willow rods,
the hide of a bullock and sealed with tar.

Sculled, yet it's the heft of the ocean
that carries you, adrift as Saint Brendan,
sped or eddied by its whim.

You are a swimmer, purling under the water,
muffled outsweep and insweep,
beyond my reach, a single fish

yet called to a shoal,
pushed out by the clang of a lighthouse bell,
drawn in by salt on your lips.

You are the furthest shore,
crackled with periwinkle shells,
torn kelp and the sigh of a winter storm.

Turner's flight

Fishermen at sea, 1796 by JMW Turner

As a youth he learned
how watercolours spill
through canvas grain and weight,
now oils shiver in his hands.
He paints the waves
clear enough to glow

yet with such thump and throw
that they could snap apart
these men upon the rocks
or upturn their craft and fill their throats:
it's a hungry skill to steer at night
and grasp the fish to string out life.

Four fishermen, hunkered in their boat,
sodden, sullen, red-raw hands yanking
at a rope or deftly parting guts
and flesh, sail unaware across
the starting line of Turner's flight
from solid land to paint with light, just light.

The sound of hot sap

trapped in a log on a fire.
What's that in English?
In Swedish we have
a term for just that noise.

Aggie and I hunt for words
like beagles in a pile of leaves.
Will my island mother tongue
- for all its honed and cadged

and nicked abundance -
have a term so tightly framed?
As I live here for longer my English
doesn't grow, my Swedish fades.

Aggie carries a melancholy,
a darkened sea from which
she comes up for bursts of light,
of laughter, like a breaching

humpback whale. Yet
I love darkness, it lets me
stop doing, sit down and be.
I'm less sure, at risk from what

I euphemistically call *flat* -
means *low. Knacka: to tap*,
courtesy of Google Translate,
no, that's not right. A pause.

Knaka, without the C, to creak.
That's it! And I see a young girl
in overlong woollen jumper,
sat hot close to a wood fire,

back tingling with the chill
of a draught, enthralled
by twirls of flame. Scent
of smoke in her nose

as she strains to hear
the tiny, repeated knock
of sap boiling out from a crack:
the tree's old life departing.

Bulgari's hands

Turns out *she does hand-modelling*
has nothing to do with clay clogged nails,
coil pots and selling for a tenner
on a trestle table, in the echoes
of a Catholic church hall.

So, Anna's adopted, her hands
moulded by a swirl of genes
from the streets of Mumbai. Skin,
the colour of Gulab Jamun, fingers
delicate and poised as ballerinas en pointe.

That's why the camera's in close-up,
her face cropped out, locked onto
the Bulgari bracelet spun on her wrist:
a fusion of culture and modernity,
mother of pearl, carnelian, lapis lazuli.

In the corner, the G4S security guard,
solid as a lump of pummelled clay,
eyes the door for strangers
and watches her to ensure this model,
paid by the scant hour, doesn't palm the prize.

A month's kisses

Gabrielle Dupont: clear chestnut eyes, trim figure, pinned up hair, puts three baguettes on the table. Just this, for her mother's watch? There's no smell of bread until she breaks a crust and presses her nose into the white. It's yesterday's batch and cheaper. She places a small lump of chocolate on Debussy's plate and finds herself scratching her wrist. The skin is red and cracked, again. He won't like that.

Debussy will be back shortly. She glances round their room, sees his second favourite jacket - the one with the purple silk lining - has fallen to the floor. As she gathers it up she notices its weight is unbalanced, a letter in the inside pocket. She recognises his handwriting - short letters, looped d's - a billet doux. But not for her.

She shouts at him. That shocks him at first, he's hardly through the door. *You viper! You use me and then*. He cuts in, *Forget it. Lilly is nothing. To say sorry to you is pointless: you can't wipe out a month's kisses or a body's caresses by passing an Indian rubber over them*. He grins at his turn of phrase, his eyes unfocus, notes already forming.

faun dreams
wandering tune
no sense of a key

Your calloused feet
Bihar State, India

I take off my boots,
place them by flipflops
curled by the sun.

In the church
the women sit
in pools of colour,

accustomed to the floor,
their feet tucked away.
A few men dawdle at the back.

How can I, who's never
farmed grit and thorn,
speak words of life?

Amva, your rose sari shines,
your hands have cut wheat,
smoothed walls with cow dung,

strung out a line of kids.
You pray in Magahi for my son
who's sick, in distant England.

How beautiful are your
simple calloused feet,
you who live good news.

So much depends

         upon our hungry daggers held wide,
    his onyx eyes watch me
daring me to strike his flesh
    to out-tumble fate.
      Can I, Young Siward,
        fresh to this art and tribe,
          unseat this man
              who's drenched with such blue blood?
            He feints a blow and spits
           Thou wast born of woman,
                I wheel and
                stumble like a fool,
           but swords I smile at.
        Macbeth knows the way this plays:
                I must die
           like a white chicken
              so I cut inside
            his guard
            and catch him full in the ribs.

    Shift to Jackie's candled room,
        digs in the red light zone,
            he wears a leather jacket,
          Heineken beside him,
     insouciant.
       We're taking Equus
  to play the Edinburgh Fringe.
Are you in?
    So much depends

  the water flows undisturbed
            or breaks and I've an earring
lattice of engineering lectures   Modern History

    prudent coat   glazed with rain
                          swearfree friends
                                          and Drama
                            batik shirt hung long
              a Banquo to my name.

                                  Could there be a me?
                                  So much depends.

Poem in conversation with William Carlos Williams' poem 'So Much Depends Upon a Red Wheelbarrow'

Hour upon the stage

My line: *No. I'm her godson.*
The nurse glances up,
only next of kin are allowed.

She tucks a lock of hair into her ponytail.
You can see her, this time. But not again.
It's standard procedure.

Official lines on the whiteboard:
Felicity Anderson. Ark Royal Ward.
Puree of level 2 fluids. Hearing aids please.
Hoist A02 into tilt-in-space chair.

Your lines from life:
disingenuous Russian to slip your minder in Moscow;
English that spun a tale for me - the Young Pretender
fleeing like a spider kiting the heather;
sun-slowed ripples of French near Bordeaux.

Now is the play's anti-climax: wisps of words,
your voice retreating into your throat.

It half sinks in, even as I read
you a poem, stumbling my flow.

A blessing whispered,
a kiss blown, childlike,
from my hand.

Strange fish

Stamp collectors are a strange

silent, fish-like breed, said Orwell.
But who's breeding them
and why? Ethel, owner
of Beloved But Battered Books,
needs a few to stand
sentinel near Romance,
and Unsolved Crime.
They will model
the quiet she adores
yet still unsettle a thief
and interrupt his trickery.
For book theft
is where the semi-comic
and serious money
is these days.
Not in narcotics, fraud
or click-quick cyber-sabotage.
A bent-eared Enid Blyton
with edges wobbled by rain
- and a torn page 23 traced
with browning stickless sellotape -
will cause an oligarch to gasp:
I must have this book!

Stamp collectors are
a fish-like breed:
able to breathe underwater;
moving with just a flick;
hardly needing sleep but staring
goggle-eyed through the darkest hours,
wafting to and fro.

Stamp collectors are a breed:
one last group that won't fight back,
too introvert and kind, they're still fair game.
Stampcollectorphobe's too long a word to use in court
so raise your verbal shotguns, guys, take aim.

There's no smoke for the fool

who lives in a glasshouse
but gathers no moss.
He's stuck, parched, wilting
and mimes to each passerby
through panes stippled with algae
that he's frustrated
by forever tending tomatoes.
Oh how he longs to inhale
the finest smouldering sphagnum.

—

A workman, bad as he is blind,
always a fag in his hand
has sawed, spliced
and hammered for weeks
to build this catapult.
King or not, he cannot stand
his one-eyed neighbour.
Hurling these stones
will make that clear.

—

Familiarity breeds time
under the warmth
of a red incubation bulb:
splicing globules of seconds
with a Sheffield Steel scalpel
till they coalesce
into whole Sunday afternoons.
Each strand sags like spaghetti
made by too many cooks.

—

Many hands make light
before a fall. Young women
with singed leather gloves
gather each particle
of fizzing star spawn.
They set the cliffline ablaze
so no-one tumbles over -
for the seas have not yet been filled
to swallow their pride.

Neptune's Horses

Neptune's Horses by GF Watts (England) 1886-7

The wind tricked us.
We, who as ocean, stretched
from tropic to pack ice,
surface to light abandoned gloom.

She spoke of things we had not
touched or smelt or drunk,
curdled us until we rose
and surged towards the east.

The seafloor climbed, imperceptibly
at first, but now at pace we're squeezed
until we cannot keep our space
but curl, twist and breathe,

snort, stare and
thunder down our hooves,
crushed into a corner by the sky,
we pitch and thrash

and hurl our spray to drown
the beach and claim it ours
but - fall, slip and sink
into the salt-drenched sand.

A dragon loves

On the horizon,
beyond this tree clad valley,
lies a mountain range,
crumpled as morning bedsheets,
pale blue as if undecided
between a life as rock or sky.
If he could throw off
the deep enticement of sleep,
shake free his limbs
and centuries of blending in
the Peloponnese Dragon would rise
once more into the sky,
glittering with iridescent
pastel scales, breathing out
wreaths of cloud, veined with storm.
He would turn south in search
of sails and ships and ports
to consume with waves of fire.
Soon all would be ash and gloom.
But, dear reader, before you
scuttle underground to hide,
remember this and breathe:
the dragon *loves* his sleep.

Not what they seem

Zomba market, Malawi

Oranges are a myth,
the air is dull with dust,
tired flies stick to the wall.
Then one day they're real:

Naranja, the woman calls,
good price for you.
She sets out her fruit
in pyramids of four.

Naranja, a Bantu word
of local stock, soaks
its phrase: *naranja nanga
nili nabwino*. But,

when I lift one, I catch
a hint of salt, an Arab
dhow slipping the wind,
the mate hawking nāranj pips

into the blue. And beyond,
faint as an ant's heartbeat:
China's narang groves
covering their traces with mist.

Love, hate, punctuate

Punctuator, with a plosive p,
you detonate sandbars of text,
sweep oceans to harness sound,
tune the up-swelling tide.

Some want freedom from rules,
sails unleashed to haste
uncharted into the maelstrom
of open sea or crackling rocks.

But you take punctum, Medieval
Latin point, a gift from the tip
of a quill to guide and enhance
the jig and swirl of the word.

Your colon or semi-colon,
captains cannot make the choice,
apostrophes are worse - sailors
scatter them like battered dice -

yet phrases swing as hammocks
on your comma hooks, quotation marks
add gravy to the spoken meat,
ellipses are lime to keep us scurvy free.

You give us order with your full stop,
the bloated glutton of grammar,
adrift with port and slumping camembert:
a cannonball that sinks each ship of the line.

Perukes and periwigs

Taciturn Mr Turner
has garrulous roots
in a barber's shop in Covent Garden.
The more the clients talk
the less the boy does.
So clippings from actors'
and artists' tales, both
florid and dark,
fall into his sketches
and pulse his passion.

His father's success
is a gift of the word,
the smile and the blade,
powder and salves,
modish perukes
and periwigs:
fashion and flair.

But taste flicks.
Aristocrats in
revolutionary France
suddenly want
to blend with the crowd:
ditch wigs, wear hats
and natural hair.

England follows suit,
the business tumbles.
So Turner learns
to live by his art:
walk for his trade,
read the market,
charge three shillings a piece.

Do we fight
Wallingford 1646

for a city king,
blurred head on coin,
or for our harvests in
and no more burning crops?

My broad hands, trained
for casting millet seeds
and scything in the yield,
now clasp a musket.

This hefty gun
has ritual steps
like liturgy in church:
lead ball, black powder,

prime, ram, present.
But even when my musket
gets to fire its sulphurous load,
the shot sails high,

- more grief to pigeons
than to parliamentary men,
most of whom I know.
Thomas the brewer,

a man of thin beer,
Robert from beyond the copse
and William the fellmonger
whose word I trust.

Not all gunshots miss:
our screams are real.
Those leaders fight with words,
our bodies break and yield.

Fellmonger: a dealer in sheepskins

Breeze blocks for a heart

Vanishing Point

Qatar

An in-between place:
time-shunted,
sleep-silted.

Beyond endless glass
Doha City is skyscrapers
slicing through brown haze.

Is it too late -
as I listen for a call slipped
between Arabic and Urdu
- to abscond?

To merge into this airport
of light, huge bags of *Celebrations*,
leaking toilets.

A Porsche is parked across the atrium:
crouching, frost-coated cat
that snarls success. An Indian man

with a frayed shirt collar
hoovers the carpet in the mosque,
weaving through prostrate prayers.

Next stop Darfur, warzone.
I'll be unwelcome.
A place one could disappear.

Apart
Darfur, Sudan

This drop of calm within a war
stirs me to paint. Leaves
tousled by a cursory breeze,
the way the azure sky evaporates
to furnace white. I'd sketch

the Brown Snake Eagle
cutting high above, changing
her path with the subtlety of smoke,
but not the walls. When we've shared
tarpaulins, jerrycans and soap

with those who've fled with just
the dust between their toes,
we come here. Behind concrete walls
strung with a lash of barbed wire.
We crave a place that's safe

when twisted pickup trucks
lie burned to jet beside the road,
but at what cost? How can you greet
through a blank steel gate, swap
a smile with a kid if you're not

on the path, be known if no-one
comes to eat? Like circles of oil in water
we stay close and keep our grab-bags
near to hand. We're too few for company,
words as stale as weeviled rice.

A text arrives from home with news:
twirling kite, cushion mended,
son's scuffed knees. Meanwhile I know
the *Janjaweed* are somewhere, somewhere
in the desert gunfire strafes the night.

The Janjaweed are a brutal Arab militia active in Sudan.

Translating into Russian

Jon Hopkins Concert, Royal Albert Hall

Wires, black as apocalyptic rain
-diesel from a perforated sky -
pour from the majestic roof,
slice through lighting gantries
yet never reach the floor
but burn in rising sound.

With waves across the violins,
rumbling in the guts of timpanis
the music stokes in me, an ache.
What if the Tchaikovsky Concert Hall
also resounded to this piece
and Putin overcame his fear

of closeness to a crowd
- his long-handled spoon approach to life?
Could he sit immersed in rippled grace
but still stay locked within his skull
with breeze blocks for a heart?
Would the tunes transfer or carry

so much Western freight they
could not reach his Russian soul?
Putin favours *'Of our own – Rachmaninov'*.

Give me a child

Nadia, chipped front tooth,
crouches as close as she dares
to a sputtering gas burner,
her left leg trembles.
Where's Dad?
Distant voice of a Russian shell.

Rewind to Putin, alone on stage,
in the cream polo-neck jumper
of a talkshow host.
Two hundred thousand Russians
waving red, blue and white,
some bussed in, some true.

Further back: Agent Viktor sips a slick
of raw quail's egg from a mug,
FC Spartak Moscow, tries not to gag,
pauses ten beats for poison.
No spasm, so sends a glass flute
upstairs to the President.

Yeltsin, cream-moulded hair,
pours his smile over
an apparatchik, a neat man
at the margin of the hall,
blue cardboard folder under his arm
to carry his notes.

Stop: breeze block room,
sputtering gas burner
and a tin sink crammed in,
its surface so cold
Putin's boyish hand sticks.
Rats that terrify the dogs.

Instinct

    I need one now,   President Trump orders   *I need one now!*
The boy is tethered to his Mum   American troops out of Syria,

    but strains towards the ground.   the Kurds find out on Twitter.
    Turkey bursts in with tanks, *I'll give you one later* she says,

    130,000 people scatter. he ought to be at pre-school,
she needs to clean the sinks. In Tal Abyad glass lacerates the air, Ana screams

    and holds her father tight.   On the ground
    is a tiny orange dot,   It was Donald's choice alone.

    a spent and grimy sweet.

Wrapped

A grid: haze of smoky shifting greys.
Beyond, below, sliced line, railway leads to a cluster of carbon
black, smoke stacks,
factories to manufacture what? Target got for bomber just turned
nineteen, Jack, cold as ice-packed cod, pupils wide, nerves shot,
each ack-ack blast judders Lancaster bolts, will be their last,
cannot see
for smoke and grit and tears, jerks the lever
and she drops
smooth
steel
wrapped.

Swaddled.
The siren shrieks shredding
thought, caught in the hall, no shelter
in this part of town, Marlena dives
under stairs, squeezes up, scent-close
to the sweet stack of pine, her winter fuel
jerks to try to close the door
squeaks to a halt, will not budge,
cradles Uli between her knees,
her hands, her face
holds tight.

An Afghan flight: a drone on 'seek'
tapered
bleak
no windows
there's no-one in but in a Houston room, Jack, just turned
nineteen, ice cubes floating in his coke
a paler line and kicks of dust, militia men he thinks for sure, target
won, button pressed
Larmina rests

against a wall
head swathed
 missile sent
  baby Aina
  held close
  time's up.
    Shift
  wrapped.

Checkpoint

Bethlehem, Palestinian Territories

Is this the place where
Christ first breathed:
sucking air into his flat lungs,
taking in life?

Smattering of sheep,
stony hill, bent tree.
Bethlehem's on pilgrims' lips
but it's still poor.

Dusk stains the sky pink.
I see below my window
the street fill with youth
heading to my right,

hands curled on rocks,
half concealed.
Today Talib, the roofer, was beaten
at the checkpoint.

They hurl their stones
at the neat Israeli guards
crouched behind sandbags,
shades and toughened glass.

Later, down in Manger Square,
I buy a tea set
in a tourist shop.

Each pewter cup
when filled with tea
is too hot to touch.

This teetering moment
A camp in Poland

when atoms in each
trampoline spring squeal
as they're wrenched apart until

snap! Recoil shoves gravity
out of the way,
rockets potential into kinetic,
and propels you,

lopsided smile with missing tooth,
scattered freckles, braided hair
- the colour of the wheat
outside Mariupol -

hazel eyes wide
with the thrill of safe fear,
looking into Mummy's eyes
as she smiles from her thin face,

Look at me! Look at me!
trying to hold your gaze
so you forget, in this moment,
the space where Daddy would be.

Tantalising flame

In their wake

Last week, the magnolia
was an exuberant stroke,
bold and bright
against a powder blue sky,
each flower fat with life-lush pink,
air soaked with its earthy scent.

And now, as its petals curl,
and dry to crumpled beige and fall,
I feel I'm walking in the pause
that follows God and Adam's evening stroll,
the grass in their footprints
still bending back to shape.

On the cusp
Monasterio de Leyre

A soft light falls
on each monk lost
or puzzled in prayer.
Columns of stacked
limestone stretch up
into the dark.

The light provides
a hint of nurture
for these ten men
in simple folded black,
reflects from bald heads,
suffuses grey hair.

Chanted notes of Matin
pulse and fade.
The monks bow deep
before the glory of God,
don't notice a tourist:
I'll pass, a flicker and gone.

One monk, late thirties,
olive eyes. Why's he here?
Acting work that made
his heart beat fast
but came and went?
The touch, and go, of God?

Later he sits, leant
against the outer wall,
head in a slim book.
At the boundary
in the fresh or swirling wind.
On the edge, alone.

What lies ahead

Water slides, skips, jumps
this mountain's slopes,
she's careless and headlong:
an exuberant child.
Bubble white, bursting
with oxygen, she slips
into sparkling jets then
tumbles, falls, splashes,
gathers for moments
in a shallow pool -
clean as a cloudless sky,
hexagons of wobbling sun -
tips over an edge,
coils helter skelter,
cascades, onward,
downward, fast, free.

Careless and headlong
as a child that can't foresee
twisting an ankle:
drawing breath in algal sludge,
clogging with plastic bags
and split lager cans,
dribbling through drought.

Or else perceive she'll bask, wrapped in waterweed,
flirt with iridescent dragonflies,
yield to the tips of a willow's caress,
until, at last, she slides into the arms of salt and sea.

Still point

Driven fast by the wind,
a boat with ochre sail
tilts towards the storm,
is twitched to a line

by a brine-seasoned skipper.
Amid the thrash
of the waves, she holds
an intersection of thirds:

active space balanced
by a flick of a gull, a point
at the centre of the dance,
teasing the fray of the light.

Still life?

This orange has been failing
since it was plucked,
its umbilical cord of sap,
snapped.
I cut into its skin,

peel back the hide.
Is it still? For the flesh
yields a spiked taste
with a pulse of faintly
remembered heat.

Every inch of its surface
is pockmarked, its shape
still plump, no sheen of mould
but it holds those spores.
So is it, still, life?

We gasp at a dutch
Still Life with Fruits,
so lush the juices bleed
just as the food tilts
beyond return

yet we cast out a fruit
that starts to fade.
For it proclaims,
in sharp citric notes,
what it is to be still life.

Lasting Difference

At the end of a tube of blunted white
is a twig without leaves or sap.
Safe from the tug of a roe deer's teeth,
from the powdered brush of a moth's wing
and the hoot and retort of Tawny owls,
who once roosted here. The plant never grew.

I step back and see the tube is one
of many, each solid polypropylene,
in a 2m grid, row upon row. Six saplings,
out of hundreds, have broken free
from the top of their protective shells
and spill with fresh beech leaves.

I've walked my footprints deep
into this land, this North Downs ridge.
It once tumbled with life: beech, birch,
yew and ash splattered with sunlight,
ground perforated by badger sets,
purple spotted orchids shy in a glade.

The Forestry Commission wants order.
It's tempting. *Commercial viability,*
efficient harvesting of natural resources:
each Latinate word cowed and controlled,
syllables chained like logging trucks.
But nature is not neat, it's interlaced.

In 30 years these tubes will still be here:
semi-crystalline, rigid, proof against the sun.

Can we not pray

because it's too bold,
our words crumble,

or faith's a can,
crush-cast in the nettles?

We can't seem to settle
for a concrete or lost God.

Odd, when we
reject his rule,

cast out our sin
by blocking out the word,

unheard. When we pause,
if we pause,

is the thought of God
caught like a roe deer

at the edge of a copse
before she leaps?

Although we do not pray
we stumble by

when breathing's feint
and stutter out its husk

to halt our slide,
till we no longer speak

for fear we'd leak
great streams of faith.

Let there be lights
'Sower of the Systems' by George F Watts, 1902

God is moving fast. Striding
through tunnels of firmament
like a coal-miner setting
charges of dynamite. Living
brave as sparks scratch at methane,
tantalising flame.

His robe flares with moonlight,
scything off galaxies in curls.
Watts has shattered the Sistine
Chapel with its coiffured God
and self-absorbed Adam,
hardly bothered to receive life.

Watts' divine has a pulse
and a pace. A day's not long
to crack the void and scatter
stars. The artist, a master
of faces, the holy and the myth,
frees his brush to paint

the unpaintable, *the great
vesture into which everything
that exists is woven*. Thus he casts
seeds for Kandinsky's symbols,
Vorticism's lines of speed,
Hodgkin's celebrations of the stroke,
and faith and doubt and room for both.

Beauty for ashes

Intertwined

Rosebuds slowly unfold
like words from your first date
at the corner caff with Joan.
Their candelabra rise
above the garden soil
that you tilled, made rich.

At the village edge
the land is thick
with meadow grass;
ox-eye daisies grow
like fried eggs on stalks.
The air twitches with pollen.

Three short rose bushes
on the slight curved rise
of your grave, their leaves dark
against the tan earth.
The jam jar is dry
and drifted with dirt.

A blackbird's dropping
has smeared your headstone
down through your middle name.
Joan spits on a tissue
and gently clears it
like lipstick from your cheek.

She tips the watering can -
gunmetal grey
from a time before
all things were plastic.
Thin streams of water fall,
watering you, the gardener in the soil.

Helix and the Quirk

"The capacity to blunder slightly is the real marvel of DNA. Without this special attribute, we would still be anaerobic bacteria and there would be no music."
- Lewis Thomas

    her curls spall
               untended
                                    his cheeks
                    sag like woollens on a washing line
  I'm working class
came down from Leeds
  everyone in Bemerton knows me
                    I've no imagination
                          but paint just what I see
              I'm not afraid of the dark
  husband left me
for a younger woman on heat
    the usual story
                    unruffled double bed
                        no sign of a wife
                  grief fled
    totters as she turns
breath flinging
    fire-water
                  mushroom soup
                          tea

        semi-quaver

Seen
Delhi

One drop of juice
slides down the side
of a scrap of melon.
It pauses - on the cusp -

then finally falls onto
a woman's tongue.
Her bed is the earth
behind the third oil drum.

She stumbles up and off
through veils of diesel fumes,
belching car horns and shoves
to an arched temple, steadies,

takes a grass brush in her left hand
and sweeps the dust
in the measured loops of a dance.
Her eyes are chalk white.

Later, as the thumping heat fades,
she feels the walls
for sandstone, sapphire, jade:
fingertips sipping the colours.

Her footsteps fall, shy as a secret.

Through silence

let the words linger
    like blueberries on your tongue
        twist and tumble them

                pray simply
                      fresh as a kid's smile
                          for those of halting talk

                entrance God's ear
            as much as those
            with waltzing speech

    released from your lips
to trip slip swim
    take a word and give it spin

                keep public prayers short
                          close the shutters
                    whisper in your hand

            tone inflexion and intent
        merge them with others
             like bubbles of thought

        no babble
    fluid wrought
        for you will be heard

                eddied not caught
            through silence
              spoken

Girl in a headscarf
East Belfast

She tries to stand
on shiny rollerblades.
As her slim hands
grasp the wall,
the bricks abrade
her fingertips.

Beige Muslim headscarf
falls loosely round her face.
She steadies, waits, pushes off
down Dunvegan Street
- rammed tight with
two-up two-downs -

past a painted mural:
two balaclavaed men,
stocky and distorted,
hold Kalashnikovs
to claim this land
for the UVF.

I catch the girl's eye and wonder
if it's a trespass
to exchange a glance.
She half smiles,
pulls herself up to a narrow door,
flaps the letterbox, arrives home.

After your wheelchair

it's your feet I notice most:
white as cooked chicken,

bare despite November chill.
Are you going down to the sea?

Can I lean on you? Your eyes are kindled
with light. Your blouse: a splash of tulips.

You pour joy, I say.
Or tears, you reply.

You rise cautiously from your chair,
like a sea anemone opening to the tide,

grasp the left arm strap
of my backpack and shuffle behind me.

We thread between rock pools
and seal-smooth boulders of shale.

*Don't stand on the green rocks,
they're slippery.* We reach

the water's cusp. You stand
for a few moments holding my wrist,

your ankles sloshed by the waves.
A pause, then *we'd better go*.

What caught me out

A board-rubber in flight is a terrifying thing.
Strip of felt clasped in 6 inches of varnished beech
- flung from on high as if to crack an off stump.
It twisted as it hurtled past, crashed into the floor
with an outburst of white chalk dust,
skidded 10 feet and slammed into the far wall.

Concord was the first word Father Byrne taught us,
trying to make Latin sync with life in the 80's.
To that cone-nosed jet with its isosceles wings,
its chest-filling roar. He drilled *amo, amas, amat*
and, best of all, his *amabunt!* hollered
with all his frame and joy in plosive sound.

The day when Collins' backchat snapped
Father Byrne's restraint, caused him to hurl
the board-rubber to miss and shock,
became a key part of my picture of the man.
Six feet four in his polished black brogues,
a priest who loved Latin, who you would not cross.

Until he went and died. I wouldn't be surprised
if his heart gave out, he was far from lean.
We filed into his funeral in the old Assembly Hall.
I didn't feel much until caught out as we sang
his favourite hymn *Thank you Father for giving us
your Son*, lyrics of a humble, grace-blown heart.
I glimpsed behind the stature of the man,
beyond one moment and a scanty cartoon.

Cracked

You could pass Ruth,
perhaps notice
the auburn strands
in her long grey hair,
but miss the way she looks.

Clare, young brunette with Zac,
curled up in his car seat,
dipped into a moment of sleep
and smashed into Ruth's car,
snapping her neck,
vertebrae wrecked.

Ruth survived, spent the winter
held in a halo traction brace,
bolts pushing onto her head.
Press charges? *Of course not.*
Clare was worn out, I know what
it's like to be a mum.

Ruth plants Perovskia,
an aromatic Russian Sage,
at the edge of her garden:
tiny tubular flowers
in whorls of lavender blue
to scent each passerby with light.

Acknowledgements

- 'Daughter, Wandering' shortlisted in the Wells Festival of Literature Poetry Competition, 2024
- 'Turner's flight' first published in *Acumen*, 106
- 'Bulgari's hands' first published in *Poems Worth Hearing*, Episode 17
- 'A month's kisses' first published in *Time Haiku*, Issue 59
- 'Your calloused feet' first published in the *Hidden Light*, Mole Valley Poets
- 'There's no smoke for the fool' long-listed for the Canterbury Festival Poet of the Year, 2022
- 'Neptune's horses' first published in *The Ekphrastic Review*, 2022
- 'A dragon loves' first published in the *Down to Earth*, Mole Valley Poets
- 'Perukes and periwigs' first published in *South Magazine*, 70
- 'Do we fight? published in *Dreamcatcher*, Issue 46 and Writing on Air Festival Nov/Dec 2023
- 'Vanishing point' first published in *New Contexts: 6*, 2024
- 'Apart' first published in *Shooter Literary Magazine*, Summer 2022
- 'Give me a child' first published in *Poetry Worth Hearing*, Episode 21
- 'Wrapped' shortlisted in the Bangor Poetry Competition 2022
- 'Checkpoint' first published in *Sky Island Journal*, Issue 42
- 'In their wake' first published in *Poetry Worth Hearing*, Episode 20
- 'What lies ahead' first published in *South Magazine,* 70
- 'Let there be lights' first published in *The Ekphrastic Review*, 2022
- 'Intertwined' first published in the *'Shrouded in Silence'* Exhibition for the Brigitte Trust
- 'Helix and the Quirk' first published in *New Contexts: 6*, 2024
- 'Seen' first published in the *Hidden Light*, Mole Valley Poets
- 'What caught me out' first published in *Frogmore Papers*, 105

About the author

Richard Lister is a poet who invites you into stories of intriguing characters, places and images. He enjoys enabling people to further develop their poetry through running engaging workshops and creative coaching.

He is a poetry competition judge and Corresponding Editor for the *Frogmore Papers* and his work is published in 13 international magazines such as *Acumen*, *Orbis* and *The Ekphrastic Review*. He has lived and worked across the UK, in Cambodia during a civil war and in Malawi in Africa.

www.ingramcontent.com/pod-product-compliance
Lightning Source LLC
Chambersburg PA
CBHW051553010526
44118CB00022B/2690